trash texts

Marion Wolters

Мадера

Часть первая

Дети со смехом бегают по деревянным скамейкам, которые установлены на террасированном поле, которое больше не возделывается.

Алина, Хорхе, Гастон и Лейла из импровизационного театра «Comunicate Einfach» сидят в первом ряду.

Вы вовремя получили «го».

FSC
www.fsc.org
MIX
Papier aus ver-
antwortungsvollen
Quellen
Paper from
responsible sources
FSC® C105338

Herstellung und Verlag: BoD – Books on Demand,
Norderstedt
ISBN: 9783758311642

ALINA GASTON LEILA JORGE

Estate

Mezzogiorno

La roccia vulcanica calda vaporizza quando qualcuno ci cammina sopra e rovescia gocce di una bevanda.

Il profumo del mare si fonde con la bellezza blu cobalto di un giorno di risveglio. La libertà sta al di sopra della celebrazione dei colori, che è fatta di rosso vibrante, verde vivido e giallo solare.

Jorge rappresenta il potere della decisione in quel giorno.
Alina rappresenta la volontà di portare a termine qualcosa.
Gaston incarna il desiderio di creare qualcosa di nuovo.
Leila e Garston rappresentano il magnetismo della bellezza.

L'azzurro del cielo, il colore della involontarietà si si chiede sulle ambizioni degli artisti del teatro d'improvvisazione "Communicate EinFach" e assiste teso e incantato.

In questa scena, Jorge canta in sottofondo solo per il pubblico ciò che Gaston sta pensando e provando.

Si avvicina lentamente a Leila. "Gaston?", lei sorride. Lui annuisce.

Jorge: "È cambiata molto".

Dopo una breve chiacchierata, Leila chiede: "Come sta tua moglie?", toccando il dolore di Jorge. Con cautela attraversano la calda roccia vulcanica fino al bar della spiaggia.

Parole chiave del pubblico: fenicottero, respirativ

Gaston: "Sono vedovo". Leila ascolta in silenzio. C'è bellezza nell'accettazione del suo dolore.

Jorge: "Mi chiedo se smetterò mai di sentire la perdita di mia moglie. È così bello avere Leila che mi ascolta".

Un fenicottero si unisce a loro.

Leila: "Domani devo incontrare degli amici per una piccola festa estiva. Tu vieni?

Gaston: Sì, grazie!

Mi sento come non mi sono mai sentito prima. Denominerò questo nuovo stato con una parola appena inventata "respirativ."

Parole chiave del pubblico: equivalente, woudrage

Una sera d'estate nel giardino di una villa. L'unica decorazione è una fontana di pietra consumata dalle intemperie. I conoscenti di Leila accolgono subito Gaston nella loro cerchia.

Su un tovagliolo vede un segno politico che conosce.

Leila: "Molte cose qui devono essere viste con una certa distanza dai fenomeni familiari". Un conoscente saluta Leila e le presenta un amico.

Jorge: "È davvero equivalente? Non credo che."

Gaston va al vecchio pozzo di pietra dove non c'è acqua. Una zanzara si posa sul suo polso. La lingua del camaleonte seduto sul bordo del pozzo di pietra la cattura. Crea una nuova parola francese: woudrage.

Conosco il politico che è appena arrivato. Oh, no. La scritta sul tovagliolo corrisponde esattamente alla sua posizione politica.

Invierno

Noche

Liason et cohabitation

Tierra y frío conviven en el planeta Tierra. Sólo puedes moverte muy despacio sobre la superficie resplandeciente, cuyos cristales de nieve individuales son transparentes. Pero el invierno en el planeta Tierra no tiene la misma forma en todas partes.

Para probar: Estar en la nieve. Construir una morada con ramas, nieve y otros materiales y permanecer en ella. Acoger situaciones aparentemente inhóspitas y sentirse cómodo en ellas. Imagina cómo el frío expulsa la inflamación del cuerpo.

Las señales del público se esparcen por la arena y son leídas por turnos por dos compañeros del público.

Palabra clave del público: carretilla

En un desierto del planeta Tierra, comienza el invierno. Camellos sin cuidadores se dirigen a una oscura formación de piedras. La meten en una enorme carretilla, que también yace allí. Un día y una noche después está completamente llena. Animales desconocidos deambulan entre las rocas.

Palabras clave del público: tren costero, compras,

Los camellos no tienen misión, así que se dan una misión a sí mismos: quieren conectar dos oasis en el desierto como un tren costero que conecta varios lugares de la costa. La pesada carga no es una carga.

Una carga ligera como después de una estimulante tarde de compras en otras partes del planeta por parte de los habitantes de la Tierra. Tener muchas cosas maravillosas en su equipaje y estar contentos de haber conseguido una u otra cosa que necesitaban o que no necesitaban mucho más barata.

Palabras clave del público: Kalauer, Rock Planet, Bolsa.

Los camellos llevan la carretilla a una zona restringida del gobierno. Les dejan entrar. No es lugar para calcos, sino para investigaciones y descubrimientos secretos. ¿Son las piedras de un planeta rocoso? Un hallazgo que, de llegar al público mundial, causaría turbulencias en los mercados bursátiles

Señal del público: enamorarse.

Los camellos también ven la palabra "enamorarse" entre las piedras y se enamoran.

夏秋

晡

夏末的温暖弥漫在身体里。培养体育活动，实验和短途旅行。行动中的生动活泼。

尝试一下：想象一下，身体的每个细胞是如何被太阳能激活的，并导致刚刚被激活的想法的详细实施计划。

三名宇航员在即兴剧院"沟通EinFach"中从太空观看，该剧院播放了他们过去的场景。她给了他关键词

"北京，温室，嘈杂，协约国，你所看到的"

在他们离开之前，希望有一个散文版本：

三名宇航员正在为首次太空飞行做准备。除了每天从太空协会获得的训练外，他们还每周额外留出两个小时进行慢跑和力量训练。根据季节的不同，太阳不再那么热，即使在午休时间也可以进行运动。

不要忘记他们国家的协约国，三名宇航员应该在飞行中学习其他两个国家的语言，直到初学者水平结束。他们将花费一小部分专业时间，并从飞行的第三周开始用对方的母语相互交流。

在游览过程中，他们将在其他宇航员在奥里亚拉星球上建造的温室中进行从未尝试过的植物实验。在他们以前从未经历过的变化中着迷。他们的身体已经为此进行了艰苦的训练，这一点显而易见。

没有日光会是什么样子，如果你失重几周会是什么样子？他们能否在环球飞行中认出北京？他们随身携带乐器，并乐于一起创造悦耳的音调和嘈杂声。

Madeira, Primavera, Segunda Parte

Manhã

Duas raparigas estão felizes a pisar as poças que a chuva deixou no relvado.

Alina dirige-se ao público:

Distribuímos folhas, canetas e cordões de algodão. Basta escreverem como querem criar a vossa primavera deste ano e pendurarem as folhas de papel com os cordões de algodão ao lado das folhas reais das árvores de seda, também conhecidas como árvores Kapokok. Depois, incorporaremos as vossas ideias na performance.”

Um homem está a tossir. "As árvores são muito altas. Como é que vamos lá chegar?"

Isto é um teatro de improvisação. Ponham em prática as vossas ideias e soluções de problemas de forma espontânea. Vocês vão pensar em alguma coisa,” Garçon motiva o público perplexo. “ Vamos apanhá-los como frutos maduros, mas talvez vocês também possam colocar as vossas fichas de ideias para que caiam no palco na altura certa,” diz ele a rir. “Começaremos depois de terem resolvido esta tarefa. ”

Algum tempo depois.

Jorge diz: “Muito bem. Vamos começar. Aqui está a primeira resposta: voar alto e cair baixo de uma só vez. Parece que isto é um excerto do vosso processo de resolução de problemas. ” O público ri-se. Alina e Jorge constroem um dragão e deixam-no subir. Ele sobe lentamente em ondas de vento. Uma folha de ideias solta-se, cai sobre o dragão, que rapidamente cai com ele. A Leila vai apanhá-lo.

Ela lê: "Estar completamente" e Garçon complementa "Na mente". Da plateia, uma modelo brasileira grita: “Nós nos concentramos na palavra ‘única’ e fazemos com que as letras individuais da palavra dancem em espírito à nossa frente. “ O público aplaude e implementa a proposta.

Jorge lança uma corda sobre o ramo mais baixo de uma árvore Kapok, que fica um pouco mais longe do palco, e sobe. Ele pega numa folha de ideias colada com o recorte de um figo de um lado e de uma laranja do outro e lê: "Desfrutar a facilidade associativa de um novo entendimento" e "Celebrate the happiness of a new understanding".

O público canta, dança, lança termos para o palco que Jorge, Leila, Garçon e Alina reinterpretam de forma lúdica. Alegria da Primavera.

Interpretationen

interpretations

interprétations

تفســـــيرات

Madeira, Primeira Parte

A ação do segundo capítulo decorre na Madeira, em Portugal, e, tal como todos os outros capítulos, está adequadamente escrita na língua local.

"As crianças correm a rir entre os bancos de madeira colocados num campo em socalcos que já não é cultivado." O "campo em socalcos que já não se cultiva" é uma referência à economia da Madeira. As encostas, entrecortadas por degraus, são utilizadas para a agricultura. Aqui são colhidas frutas europeias e tropicais, como mangas, bananas, uvas, figos, laranjas, maçãs e cereais, por exemplo. O trabalho árduo dos agricultores nos campos em socalcos contrasta com a despreocupação das crianças que correm de um lado para o outro. Ao mesmo tempo, apontam para outro sector da economia madeirense: o turismo.

Winter-spring

The motif of the second chapter is modified. The hard work of the farmers on the terraced field takes place in a successful start-up. The lightness of the children playing is taken over by nature in spring which also inspires them to play an anticipation game: "Can we effortlessly anticipate the colours and shapes of nature? Then we compare our drawings with the works of art of nature."

Été-printemps

« L'enthousiasme du nouveau départ se mêle à la soif de savoir de la bioinformaticienn. » Comme dans le deuxième chapitre, il s'agit ici aussi d'un nouveau projet de travail. On ne sait toutefois pas encore s'il sera couronné de succès comme décrit dans le deuxième chapitre: il commence tout juste à se développer. Des phrases humoristiques alternent avec des questions scientifiques et le décrivent: « La maturation des idées. »

Primaballerina, extravagant, Papagei, literarische Verzerrung, Hängebauchschwein

Auch hier geht es um etwas Neues im Arbeitsleben. Diesmal ist es jedoch weniger angenehm. Es kommt dem Protagonisten immer wieder in den Sinn, doch die rationale Einsicht, die Idee zu verwirklichen, reicht - wie so oft - nicht aus. Eine emotionale Motivation wäre notwendig, existiert jedoch nicht.

Exotische Teewelt: das was neu ist, ist angenehm. Der Protagonist ist offen und lässt sich gerne in die neue angenehme Welt mitnehmen. Ist dies ein Sinnbild des Menschseins oder unserer Zeit?

Estate

Ciò che si vede è ciò che è? Quanto è vera la propria interpretazione? Gaston incontra nuovamente Leila dopo molti anni. Leila è cambiata, ma è sempre lì per Gaston. Così lui trascua lo sguardo dalle differenze, ma queste sono sempre presenti sullo sfondo. Il nuovo ambiente lo stimola: "Crea una nuova parola francese: woudrage". Si diverte ad essere accettato: "I conoscenti di Leila accettano immediatamente Gaston nella loro cerchia". Se non fosse per la condensazione dei segni: "Sul tovagliolo vede un segno politico che conosce". Gli animali mostrano simbolicamente ciò che accade alle vittime politiche: "Una zanzara si posa sul suo polso. La lingua del camaleonte seduto sul bordo della fontana di pietra lo prende". Quanto bisogna essere attenti per evitare di diventare una vittima politica? L'accettazione della società circostante e le parole offuscanti "Molto qui va visto con distanza dai fenomeni noti" riusciranno a creare una nuova consapevolezza a proprio svantaggio? Come ci si può proteggere da questo?

Invierno

"Los camellos no tienen misión, así que se dan una misión a sí mismos...". Quizás uno ya ha pensado en esto, le gustaría utilizarlo como gancho para poner en práctica este impulso. Tal vez es sólo el tiempo y la idea correcta está ahí porque ha creado el espacio. Que es eso que tu siempre has querido hacer: mmh, ¿Qué es tu fue eso otra vez?

Automne

Ici aussi: la percée des idées, des processus, des accords. Cette fois-ci, sur le terrain diplomatique: c'est réussi!

夏-秋 - 中文

宇航员学习对方的语言，并从飞行的第三周开始用对方的母语进行交流。这个实验能否在地球上的日常职业生活中实现？这个想法蕴含着哪些经验和可能性？

宇航员会问自己 "没有日光……会是什么样子？这可以作为宇航员培训的预备行动来尝试，以了解自己是否想从事这一职业。"……也可以在午休时间进行体育锻炼"。这也是给所有想了解地球上未知宇宙的人的建议。

Madeira, primavera, Segunda Parte

Teatro de improvisação em ação. O público compete com os quatro actores do teatro de improvisação Communicate EinFach. Os exercícios de improvisação que não devem ser levados totalmente a sério estimulam a imaginação a inventar novas variações. "Para gozar a leveza associativa de uma nova compreensão".

Please feel invited

Nachfolgend drei unausgesprochene Einladungen, die dem Buch
zugrunde liegen:

Einladung zum Kennenlernen

In diesem Buch laden Sie die acht Jahreszeiten

Winter-Frühling
Frühling
Frühling-Sommer
Sommer
Sommer-Herbst
Herbst
Herbst-Winter
Winter

ein, sie neu kennenzulernen.

Die vier Elemente Feuer, Wasser, Erde und Luft wurden ihnen
zugeordnet und auch einige Eigenschaften.

Es gibt Angebote zum Ausprobieren, die fast alle in der Natur
oder einem der vier Elemente durchgeführt werden können.

Below are three unspoken invitations which are the basis of the book:

Invitation to get to know

In this book the eight seasons

winter-spring
spring
spring-summer
summer
summer-autumn
autumn
autumn-winter
winter

invite you to get to know them.

The four elements fire, water, earth and air were assigned to them and also some properties.

There are offers for trying out. Nearly all of them can be done in nature or in one of the four elements.

Einladung zum Verändern des Textformates

Diese Texte erscheinen in ungeordneter Reihenfolge.

Man kann

- die Kapitel chronologisch ordnen
- die Reihenfolge der Kapitel auf eine andere Weise anordnen
- die Texte als Vorlage für selbstgewählte Zwecke nutzen.

Invitation to change the text format

These texts appear in an unordered sequence.

Please feel free to

- arrange the chapters chronologically
- arrange the order of the chapters in a different way
- use the texts as a template for self-selected purposes

Einladung zum kreativen Ausdruck

Ein Improvisationstheater baut spontan die Stichworte des Publikums in die Handlung ein. Daher stehen die Stichworte eines imaginierten Publikums am Anfang eines Kapitels und werden dann anschließend in die Handlung eingebaut.

Welche Stichworte hätten Sie dem Improvisationstheater Communicate EinFach gegeben? Wie hätte sich die Handlung dadurch verändert?

In der Realität gibt man oft - wie im letzten Kapitel – selbst die Stichworte und beeinflusst damit maßgeblich den weiteren Verlauf der Handlung.

Viel Spaß und Vorhang auf:

Invitation to creative expression

Improvisational theatre spontaneously incorporates the keywords of the audience into the plot. Therefore, the keywords of an imagined audience are at the beginning of a chapter and are then incorporated into the plot.

Which keywords would you have given to the improvisational theatre Communicate EinFach? How would the plot have changed as a result?

In reality, as in the last chapter, you often give the keywords yourself and thus have a significant influence on the further course of the plot.

Have fun and curtain up:

Merci

Dolmetsch- und Übersetzungsdienst
Marion Wolters
Geprüfte Dolmetscherin Englisch

+++ Wirtschaft +++ Politik +++ Medien
+++ Energie +++ Literatur +++

Journalismus in der digitalen Verbreitung, 2019
journalistische Texte, textes journalistiques, journalistic texts

Fougère, verre…, 2020
biologische Themen, thèmes biologiques, biological topics

Bleuciel de Sagesse, 2021
Konnotationsvertonungen durch eine Sprachkomponistin
Connotation settings by a language composer
Sonorisation de la connotation par un compositeur de langage
Configuración de connotación por un compositor de idiomas

Emotions create a new understanding menting thoughts while
standing on a future bridge, 2021
Poems, Gedichte, poèmes, poems

Seinsqualitäten, 2022
Ein heiteres, philosophisches Theaterstück in drei Akten und
zwei Sprachen
A light-hearted, philosophical theatrical play in three acts and
two languages

Portrait, 2022
Künsterportrait/artist portrait, bilingual: German/English

Musical Immediacy, 2022

Journalismus in der digitalen Verbreitung Teil II, 2023
journalistische Texte, textes journalistiques, journalistic texts